ABSOLUTE ESSENTIALS OF ISLAM

In the name of Allāh, Most Gracious Most Merciful.
All praise be to Allāh, Lord of the Worlds,
and peace and blessings be upon His Messenger Muḥammad,
Mercy to the Worlds.

Absolute Essentials of Islam

Faith, Prayer, & the Path of Salvation According to the Ḥanafī School

Compiled by
Faraz Fareed Rabbani

based on Shaykh Amīn Jundī's
Iṣlāḥ ʿIlm al-Ḥāl

White Thread Press
SANTA BARBARA • CALIFORNIA • USA

First Edition January 2005

ISBN 0-9728358-4-9 (*softcover*)

Published by:
White Thread Press
California USA
www.whitethreadpress.com
info@whitethreadpress.com Tel: 1 805 968 4666

Distributed in the UK by Azhar Academy Ltd. London
sales@azharacademy.com Tel: +44 (208) 534 9191

Library of Congress Cataloging-in-Publication Data

Jundī, Amīn ibn Muḥammad, 1813 or 14–1878.
[*Iṣlāḥ ʿilm al-ḥāl.* English]
Absolute Essentials of Islam: faith, prayer, & the path of salvation according to the Ḥanafī school / compiled by Faraz Fareed Rabbani.— 1st ed.
p. cm.
ISBN 0-9728358-4-9 (softcover : alk. paper)
1. Islam—Customs and practices. 2. Islam—Rituals. 3. Islam—Doctrines. 4. Hanafites. I. Rabbani, Faraz Fareed. II. Title.
BP184.J8613 2004
297–dc22
2004025997

Printed and bound in the United States of America on acid-free paper. The paper used in this book meets the minimum requirement of ANSI/NISO Z39.48-1992 (R 1997) (Permanence of Paper). The binding material has been chosen for strength and durability.

Photograph of tilework of Bursa Green Mosque by Dick Osseman
Cover design by F Ahmad
Book design by ARM

Verily, by the remembrance
of Allah do hearts find rest

—The Qur'ān 13:28

TRANSLITERATION KEY

ء (إ أ) ' (A slight catch in the breath. It is also used to indicate where the *hamza* has been dropped from the beginning of a word.)

ا a, ā

ب b

ت t

ث th (Should be pronounced as the *th* in thin or thirst.)

ج j

ح ḥ (Tensely breathed *h* sound.)

خ kh (Pronounced like the *ch* in Scottish loch with the mouth hollowed to produce a full sound.)

د d

ذ dh (Should be pronounced as the *th* in this or that.)

ر r

ز z

س s

ش sh

ص ṣ (A heavy *s* pronounced far back in the mouth with the mouth hollowed to produce a full sound.)

ض ḍ (A heavy *d/dh* pronounced far back in the mouth with the mouth hollowed to produce a full sound.)

ط ṭ (A heavy *t* pronounced far back in the mouth with the mouth hollowed to produce a full sound.)

ظ ẓ (A heavy *dh* pronounced far back in the mouth with the mouth hollowed to produce a full sound.)

ع ʿ, ʿa, ʿi, ʿu (Pronounced from the throat.)

غ gh (Pronounced like a throaty French *r* with the mouth hollowed to produce a full sound.)

ف f

ق q (A guttural *q* sound with the mouth hollowed to produce a full sound.)

ك k

ل l

م m

ن n

و w, ū, u.

ه h

ي y, ī, i

Contents

Preface

The Messenger of Allāh (Allāh bless him and give him peace) said, "Whomever Allāh wishes well for, He gives understanding of religion" (Bukhārī 71, Muslim 1037).

Allāh has commanded us to worship and obey Him with sincerity, out of reverence, love and thankfulness. Allāh says in the Qur'ān, "And they are ordered to serve Allāh only, keeping religion pure for Him, to remain upright, and to establish worship and to pay the alms-due. That is true religion" (98:5).

This worship is not possible without knowledge. This short work outlines the absolute essentials of this knowledge—in faith, prayer, and key points related to one's life and dealings. It is based on the methodology of traditional Sunni Islam according to the Ḥanafī school, the largest school of Islamic law. And its purpose is to make one's worship valid, sound, and proper in a short amount of time.

And Allāh alone gives success.

Faraz Rabbani
Amman, 2004

Belief

Allāh Most High says in the Qur'ān:

"The Messenger believes in what was sent down to him from his Lord, and the believers all believe in Allāh and His angels and His books and His messengers. We make no distinction between any of His messengers. They say, 'We hear, and we obey. Grant us Your forgiveness, our Lord. Unto You is the return'" (2:285).

The Messenger of Allāh (Allāh bless him and give him peace) said: "Whoever meets his Lord without having associated partners with Him will enter Paradise" (Bukhārī and Muslim).

Belief in Allāh

The meaning of "I believe in Allāh" is:

I accept and believe that Allāh Most High exists, is One, and that there is no god but Allāh. Allāh is the One free of need for any other, and all besides Him are in absolute need of Him, for He is the Creator and Sustainer of all things. Only He is worthy of worship, and none other deserves to be worshipped.

Allāh is characterized by all attributes of perfection, and exalted above all attributes of imperfection.

The attributes of Allāh may be classified into three categories: the personal attribute, the five negative attributes, and the seven affirmative attributes.

His **Personal Attribute** is:

Being

His **Negative Attributes** are:

Beginninglessness
Endlessness
Oneness
Self-subsistence
Absolute dissimilarity to created things

His **Affirmative Attributes** are:

Life
Knowledge
Will
Power[1]
Hearing
Sight
Speech

Allāh is absolutely unlike anything that comes to one's mind. It is not possible to understand the reality of Allāh through the intellect alone, for He is exalted above being grasped by reflection and intellect.

All other attributes return to these essential attributes, which are the most frequently mentioned in the Qur'ān.

Belief in the Angels

This is to believe in the existence of Allāh's angels. They are honored servants of Allāh, who do not disobey Him and do as they are commanded. They are not characterized by gender, nor do they eat or drink. Each angel has been given a service to perform, and among them are the higher angels and the messenger angels.

Belief in the Books

This is to believe in all the books revealed by Allāh. The main books are four: the Torah of Moses, the Psalms of David, the Gospel of Jesus, and the Qur'ān of the Prophet Muḥammad (may Allāh's blessings and peace be upon them all). Though divinely revealed, the Torah, Psalms and Gospel have been altered by men, and their laws were abrogated and superseded by the Qur'ān, which was the last revealed book. Its injunctions remain valid for all time.

Belief in the Messengers

This is to believe in the prophets and messengers of Allāh, the first of whom is Ādam (peace be upon him) and the last our Master Muḥammad (Allāh bless him and give him peace). Everything that the messengers came with is true.

Five attributes are necessary for all messengers:

Truthfulness
Trustworthiness

Conveying the message
Intelligence
Sinlessness

The opposites of these attributes are impossible for messengers. They are: lying, betrayal, not conveying the message, lack of intelligence, and sinning, whether the sins are major or minor.

Our Messenger Muḥammad (Allāh bless him and give him peace) is the best and final messenger, and the Sacred Law he came with will remain until the end of time.

Belief in the Last Day

This means believing that everyone will die, and will then be resurrected. It also means believing without doubt in:

Heaven and Hell
The Scale[2]
The Path[3]
The Questioning[4]
The Reckoning (after the Resurrection)
The Recompense (in Heaven)
Punishment (for some of the sinful), and
Torment (eternal for the unbelievers).

Belief in Destiny

This is to believe that good and evil, benefit and harm, determination and destiny are by Allāh's Knowledge, Will, Power, and Determining. The scholars mention that it means believing that what hit you would never have missed, and what missed you would never have hit.

The Rulings of the Sacred Law

In the Ḥanafī School, the actions of those morally responsible take one of eight rulings:

1. **The Obligatory** (*farḍ*) is a firm command established by a decisively established text[5] whose meaning is decisive and not open to the possibility of interpretation.

One is bound to believe in and act on the obligatory. The one who denies it could well fall into disbelief, and the one who leaves it is sinful.

If an obligatory element of an action is omitted, that action remains unfulfilled. Thus, if one omits an obligatory act of the prayer (such as a condition or integral), the prayer is invalid and unperformed.

2. **The Necessary** (*wājib*) is a firm command supported by a text that allows for the possibility of interpretation.

Denying something necessary is corruption (*fisq*), not disbelief. Leaving it is sinful.

The omission of necessary elements of the prayer does not nullify one's prayer. However, it becomes necessary to repeat one's prayer if some necessary element was omitted intentionally. If omitted absentmindedly, forgetfulness prostrations are necessary (*wājib*) at the end of the prayer. If these too were left out, then it is necessary (*wājib*) upon one to repeat one's prayer.

3. **The Emphasized *Sunna* (*sunna mu'akkada*)** is that which our Prophet (Allāh bless him and give him peace) or the Companions did most of the time and was not of worldly habits.

Leaving an emphasized *sunna* is blameworthy but not sinful. Habitually leaving such a *sunna,* however, is sinful, because it entails "turning away" from the guidance of the Messenger of Allāh (Allāh bless him and give him peace), whom we have been commanded to follow.

4. **The Recommended (*mustaḥabb*)** is that which our Prophet (Allāh bless him and give him peace) did sometimes, or was of his worldly habits.

Performing the recommended is rewarded, but leaving it is not sinful or blameworthy.

5. **The Permissible (*mubāḥ*)** in itself is neither rewarded nor punished. Such acts are rewarded, however, if accompanied by a good intention.[6]

6. **The Somewhat Disliked (*makrūh tanzīhan*)** is that which we have been commanded to leave, even though it is not sinful. The one who leaves it is rewarded, and the one who does it acted suboptimally.

7. **The Prohibitively Disliked (*makrūh taḥrīman*)** is that which we have been firmly commanded to leave through a text open to the possibility of interpretation.

Denying such a command is misguidance but not disbelief. Performing such an action is sinful.

8. **The Forbidden (*ḥarām*)** is that which we have been firmly commanded to leave, through a decisively established text.

Therefore:

The obligatory and necessary must be performed. The prohibitively disliked and forbidden must be left. It is strongly encouraged to perform the emphasized *sunnas,* and blameworthy to leave them without excuse. The recommended should be performed, and the somewhat disliked should be left. The permitted should be conjoined with good intentions, to be worthy of reward, and wastefulness should be avoided.

The way of love and slavehood entails doing everything one's Lord has commanded, whether He commanded it firmly or lightly, and avoiding everything one's Lord interdicted, whether firmly or lightly. The Messenger of Allāh (Allāh bless him and give him peace) told us, however, that the best way is to operationalize this in a gradual and steady manner. This gradual manner means that we take on supererogatory actions in a manner that is sustainable and that does not overwhelm us.

Abū Hurayra (Allāh be pleased with him) relates that the Messenger of Allāh (Allāh bless him and give him peace) said, "Verily, this religion is ease, and no one makes his religion excessively difficult except that it overcomes him. So remain steadfast, do your best, and be of glad tidings" (Bukhārī 39, Muslim 2816).

Purification (Ṭahāra)

Allāh Most High says, "And if you are unclean, purify yourselves" (Qur'ān 5:6).

And, "Allāh loves those who purify themselves" (Qur'ān 9:108).

The Messenger of Allāh said, "Purification is half of faith" (Muslim 223, Tirmidhī 3517, Ibn Māja 280).

Imam Ghazālī (Allāh have mercy on him) explained that this purification relates to the purification of the outward, which is a condition for the validity of our outward acts, and to the purification of the inward, which is a condition for the soundness of our hearts and souls.

The Ritual Bath (*Ghusl*)

The ritual bath (*ghusl*) consists of three obligatory actions:

1. Rinsing the mouth
2. Rinsing the nose
3. Washing the entire body.

One must wash everything that is possible to wash without genuine hardship, such as eyebrows, ears, belly button, mustache, the inside of the beard, and all one's hair. Women should move their earrings so that water reaches the pierced area.[7]

It is not necessary for a woman to undo her braids or ensure that water reaches all of her braided hair as long as it reaches the roots of her hair on her head. However, it is necessary for a man to undo his braids even when the water reaches the roots of his hair.

The Ritual Bath: A Detailed Description from Beginning to End

Before performing the ritual bath itself, it is an emphasized *sunna* to:

1. Begin in the name of Allāh and make the intention[8] while washing your hands up to the wrists
2. Remove filth,[9] if any, from your body
3. Wash the private parts, even if free from filth
4. Perform a complete ritual ablution (*wuḍū'*).

Then begin your ritual bath:

1. Wash your entire body three times, starting each time from the head, followed by the right side of the body, then the left, till the toes
2. It is an emphasized *sunna* to rub one's body the first time. There is no harm in using soap and the like during the ritual bath.

One should avoid the following, because they are disliked:

1. Facing the direction of prayer or supplicating during the ritual bath
2. Wasting water. (Excessive waste of water is sinful, while waste is generally blameworthy.)

Ritual Ablution (*Wuḍū'*)

Allāh Most High says,

"O you who believe! When you rise up for prayer, wash your faces, and your hands up to the elbows, and wipe your heads and (wash) your feet up to the ankles"[10] (Qur'ān 5:6).

ʿUthmān reports that the Messenger of Allāh (Allāh bless him and give him peace) said,

"Anyone who performs ritual ablution and does so well, their mistakes leave their body, even from under their nails" (Muslim).

The Obligatory Acts of Ritual Ablution

The obligatory actions of the ritual ablution are four:

1. Washing the entire face, from the top of the forehead to the bottom of the chin in length, and from earlobe to earlobe
2. Washing both arms completely, up to and including the elbows once
3. Wiping a quarter of the head above the ears once
4. Washing the feet completely including the ankles once.

The Ritual Ablution: A Detailed Description

The *sunna* way to perform ritual ablution is to:

1. Make an intention in your heart, such as, "I intend to perform ritual ablution for the sake of Allāh."[11]

2. Wash the hands up to and including the wrists.

3. Invoke the name of Allāh, such as saying *Bismi 'Llāh wa 'l-ḥamdu li 'Llāh* (In the name of Allāh, and all praise belongs to Allāh).

4. Rinse the entire mouth three times, with three handfuls of water.

5. Brush your teeth, with a tooth stick (*miswāk*) or toothbrush.[12]

6. Rinse the nose three times, with a handful of water each time. It is recommended to take water into the nostrils with the right hand and blow it out with the left hand.

7. Wash[13] the entire face. The face is defined as being from the top of the forehead to the bottom of the chin, and from earlobe to earlobe. This is the first of the four obligatory acts of the ritual ablution. It is *sunna* to wash the face three complete times. After this, pass wetted fingers through the beard if long. It is recommended to start washing from the forehead. One should avoid slapping water onto the face, as this is improper.

8. Wash your arms completely, up to and including the elbows. This is the second of the four obligatory acts of ritual ablution.

It is *sunna* to wash the arms three complete times. After this, it is *sunna* to pass the fingers through each other. It is recommended to start washing from the fingertips.

9. Wipe a quarter of the head once,[14] above the ears. This is the third of the four obligatory acts of ritual ablution. It is *sunna* to wipe the entire head starting from the top of the forehead, and recommended to also wipe the back of the neck.

10. Wipe the ears (without taking new water). It is recommended to wipe the outsides of the ears with the thumb, the insides with the index fingers and to insert the little fingers into the ear canal.

11. Wash the feet up to and including the ankles. This is the fourth and final obligatory action of the ritual ablution. It is *sunna* to wash three complete times, and to pass fingers through the toes. It is recommended to start washing from the tips of the toes, to rub with the left hand, and to pass the little finger through the toes starting with the little toe of the right foot and ending with the little toe of the left foot.

12. During the ritual ablution, it is *sunna* to observe the abovementioned order, to wash the limbs successively without undue delay, and to rub the limbs during the first washing. It is recommended to face the *qibla* throughout the ritual ablution, and to avoid splashing water onto oneself. It is improper to engage in worldly speech without need, to waste water, or to leave any of the *sunnas* without excuse.[15]

Ritual ablution is nullified by:

1. The exiting of filth (*najāsa*) or air from the private parts
2. The flowing of blood or pus from any part of the outer body, regardless of whether it comes out on its own or is made to come out[16]
3. Vomiting a mouthful or more of other than phlegm
4. Sleeping lying down, or reclining, on one's side[17]
5. Loss of consciousness
6. Loss of intellect
7. Drunkenness
8. Laughing audibly in a prayer[18] (that has bowing and prostration)
9. Intimate contact between a man and a woman, such that the private parts touch directly.[19]

The Prayer (Ṣalāt)

Abū Mālik al-Ashʿarī (Allāh be pleased with him) relates that the Messenger of Allāh (Allah bless him and give him peace) said, "Prayer is light" (Muslim 223, Tirmidhī 3517, Ibn Māja 280).

Jābir (Allāh be pleased with him) relates that the Prophet (Allah bless him and give him peace) said, "The example of the five [obligatory] prayers is like a fast stream running in front of the house of one of you in which he bathes five times daily" (Muslim 668, Aḥmad 13863).

When asked about the best of works, the Prophet (Allah bless him and give him peace) replied, "Prayer at its time" (Bukhārī 527, Muslim 85).

The outward validity of the prayer depends on the fulfillment of its obligatory conditions and integrals. Its soundness and propriety rests on the fulfillment of its necessary and *sunna* actions. The inward reality of prayer is to sincerely turn to Allāh in reverence and submission, with presence of heart and mind.

The obligatory actions in the prayer are twelve. Seven are outside the prayer, and are called conditions; five are inside the prayer, and are called integrals.

Conditions of the Prayer

The conditions for the validity of the prayer are:

1. Being in a state of ritual purity[20]
2. That one's clothes, body, and place of prayer be free of filth (*najāsa*) beyond the excused amount[21]
3. Clothing one's nakedness. For the male, this is from the navel down to and including the knees. For the female, it is her entire body except her face, her hands up to the wrists, and her feet (below the ankles)[22]
4. Facing the *qibla* (direction of the Kaʿba in Makka)
5. Knowing and believing that the prayer time has entered
6. Making an intention before beginning the prayer[23]
7. Pronouncing the opening invocation (*takbīr,* saying *Allāhu akbar*). In the obligatory prayers this must be done standing, if one is able to stand without genuine hardship.

The Integrals (*Arkān*) of the Prayer

The integrals of the prayer are:

1. Standing,[24] for those able to stand, in obligatory prayers. The minimum standing position is such that if one were to extend one's arms they would not reach the knees[25]
2. Reciting at least the equivalent of a verse of Qur'ān, whether long or short.[26] It must be noted that it is prohibitively disliked (*makrūh taḥrīman*) and sinful for the follower to recite behind the *imām,* both in loud and silent prayers
3. Bowing (*rukūʿ*), such that if one were to extend one's arms they would reach the knees

4. Prostrating (*sujūd*)
5. The final sitting, long enough to recite the *tashahhud.*

The Necessary (*Wājib*) Actions of the Prayer[27]

The necessary actions are:

1. Reciting the Fātiḥa (opening *sūra* of the Qur'ān), in (any) two *rakʿats* of obligatory prayer and in all *rakʿats* of supererogatory and *witr* prayers
2. Reciting another *sūra* or (the equivalent of) three short verses in two *rakʿats* of the obligatory prayer and in all *rakʿats* of supererogatory and *witr* prayers
3. Making this recitation of the Fātiḥa and *sūra* or verses in the first two *rakʿats* of the obligatory prayer
4. Making two successive prostrations in each *rakʿa*
5. Remaining motionless in the bowing and prostration for at least a moment[28]
6. Sitting after two *rakʿats* in a three or four-*rakʿa* prayer long enough to be able to recite the *tashahhud*
7. Reciting the *tashahhud* itself (in the first sitting, and) at the end of the prayer
8. Saying *salām* twice at the end of the prayer (adding *ʿalaykum wa raḥmatu 'Llāh* is a confirmed *sunna,* as is turning the head to the right for the first *salām,* and to the left for the second)[29]
9. The *takbīrs* of the two ʿĪd prayers (three in each *rakʿa*)
10. Reciting quietly in the Ẓuhr (noon) and ʿAṣr (mid-afternoon) prayers. The minimal valid silent recitation requires

that one pronounce the words, such that one can hear oneself.[30] The follower does not recite Qur'ān in group prayers, regardless of whether the *imām* is reciting aloud or not, though he does say all the invocations and supplications of the prayer

11. For the *imām* to recite aloud in the Fajr (dawn), Maghrib (sunset), and ʿIshā' (evening) prayers. The one praying alone has the choice of reciting aloud or quietly, as in supererogatory night prayers.

Performing the Prayer

For the prayer to be valid, certain conditions have to be met. Before one starts one must:

1. Be in a state of ritual purity, whether through the ritual bath or ritual ablution
2. Ensure purity of body, clothing, and place of prayer
3. Cover one's nakedness
4. Face the *qibla*
5. Ensure that the time of prayer has entered
6. Intend the specific prayer that one is performing and intend following the *imām* if praying in congregation.

A Complete Description of the Prayer

1. Stand, with your feet slightly apart,[31] and utter the opening invocation.[32] This is obligatory. It is necessary (*wājib*) to say, "*Allāhu akbar.*"[33] This invocation (*Allāhu akbar*) is repeated, without raising the hands, with each movement of the prayer

except when rising from the bowing (*rukūʿ*). The one leading others utters it aloud. It is recommended to keep one's gaze lowered throughout the prayer, in order to avoid distraction. When standing, this entails looking at your place of prostration.

2. Raise your hands (until level with the ears for men and to the shoulders for women) just before uttering the opening invocation, keeping the head upright throughout, and lower the hands as one pronounces the invocation. It is recommended to keep one's hands normally open, with the palms facing the *qibla.*

3. Place your right hand over your left hand (under the navel for men and on the chest for women).

4. In the first *rakʿa* only, quietly recite the opening supplication (*thanāʾ*).

5. Seek refuge from the Devil (*taʿawwudh*) quietly, in the first *rakʿa* alone, if reciting the Qurʾān in prayer. The one leading others and the one praying alone do so—as they must recite. When praying in congregation do not recite this—as one does not recite the Qurʾān behind the *imām*—unless one has missed one or more *rakʿats,* in which case one recites this when one gets up to make up the *rakʿats* missed.

6. Recite at least one verse of the Qurʾān when leading others, or praying alone. This is obligatory. When praying behind an *imām* one does not recite any Qurʾān, not even the Fātiḥa, in both loud and quiet prayers.[34]

   It is necessary (*wājib*) for the one reciting to recite the Fātiḥa, in two *rakʿats* of obligatory prayers and in all *rakʿats* of other prayers;[35] recite at least the equivalent of three short verses of the Qur'ān, in two *rakʿats* of obligatory prayers, and in all *rakʿats* of other prayers; and to make the above recitation (of the Fātiḥa and verses of the Qur'ān) in the first two *rakʿats* of obligatory prayers.

7. When leading others, recite quietly in the Ẓuhr and ʿAṣr prayers, the last two *rakʿats* of the ʿIshā' prayer and the last *rakʿa* of the Maghrib prayer, and loudly in the first two *rakʿats.*

8. Recite *Bismi 'Llāhi 'r-Raḥmāni 'r-Raḥīm* quietly before the Fātiḥa and say *āmīn* quietly after the Fātiḥa.

9. Bow. This is obligatory. The minimum bowing is that one's outstretched hands reach one's knees. It is necessary (*wājib*) to remain motionless therein, at least for a moment. It is *sunna* for women to bend until just able to reach their knees and without spreading their fingers. It is *sunna* for men to grip their knees with fingers spread out and pointing down, keeping legs and back straight and the head level with the lower back. It is recommended to keep one's gaze on the top of one's feet.

10. Recite the invocation of bowing three times. This is to say *Subḥāna rabbiya 'l-aẓīm* (Glory be to my Tremendous Lord).

11. Stand after the bowing. This is necessary (*wājib*), as is remaining motionless for a moment. It is *sunna* to say *Sami-ʿa 'Llāhu li man ḥamidah* (Allāh hears those who praise him) as you begin rising from bowing, if leading others or praying alone—followers do not say this. This is followed by *Rabbanā laka 'l-ḥamd* (Our Lord, Yours is all praise), which is said silently by the one following or praying alone—the *imām* may choose to say it silently, as well.

12. Prostrate. This is obligatory. It is necessary that one make sure to place most of one's forehead on the ground, and also the nose, both hands, knees and at least one toe of each foot. It is also necessary to remain motionless therein for at least a moment. It is a *sunna* to say *Allāhu akbar* as one begins to descend into prostration; to place one's knees on the ground first, then hands, and then the face and nose. It is recommended for men to have their hands at head level in prostration, and for women to have them at shoulder level. It is *sunna* for men to separate their abdomen from their thighs, elbows from the sides, and forearms from the ground. Women do the opposite, by keeping their abdomen close to their thighs, elbows close to their sides, and forearms on the ground, while keeping as low as comfortably possible. It is recommended to gaze towards the tip of the nose.

13. Recite the invocation of the prostration three times, saying *Subḥāna rabbiya 'l-aʿlā* (Glory be to my Exalted Lord). This is a highly emphasized *sunna.*

14. After prostrating, sit up. It is minimally obligatory to raise the head from the prostration and necessary to sit up such that you are closer to sitting than to prostration, while remaining motionless for at least a moment. The *sunna* is for men to sit on their left foot with the right foot propped up on the toes which face the direction of prayer. Women sit on their left buttock with right thigh on the left thigh and both feet coming out from the right side. It is *sunna* to place the hands on the thighs, with the tips of the fingers ending at the beginning of the knee without bending. It is recommended to keep your gaze on your thighs.

15. Prostrate a second time (as before). This is also obligatory for each *rakʿa*.

16. Stand from prostration, for the next *rakʿa*. This is obligatory. It is *sunna* to raise one's face first, then hands, and then knees. Rise on the tips of your toes without sitting after the prostration and without support of one's hands (unless out of physical need).

17. The subsequent *rakʿats* are the same as the first, except that one does not raise one's hands; one does not recite the opening supplications; nor does one seek refuge from the Devil.

18. After the two prostrations of the second *rakʿa,* sit for the first sitting, as described above. This is necessary (*wājib*). It is also necessary to recite the testification of faith (*tashahhud*). It is *sunna* to clasp one's fingers when reciting *ashhadu al lā ilāha,* with the thumb on the side of one's middle finger, and to raise the index finger; then, lower the index finger when saying *illa 'Llāh.*

19. Stand (as explained above) for the third and fourth *rakʿats* in the Ẓuhr, ʿAṣr, and ʿIshā' prayers, and only the third *rakʿa* in the Maghrib prayer. It is necessary (*wājib*) to stand up without undue delay after finishing reciting the testification of faith (*tashahhud*).

20. All actions in the third and fourth *rakʿats* are the same as the first two *rakʿats*. It is a *sunna* to recite the Fātiḥa or to say *Subḥan Allāh* three times in obligatory prayers when standing. In other prayers,[36] it is necessary (*wājib*) to recite both the Fātiḥa and the equivalent of three short verses.

21. After prostrations in one's final *rakʿa,* it is obligatory to sit for the final sitting to the extent of reciting the testification of faith (*tashahhud*) normally. It is necessary to actually recite the testification of faith completely. It is *sunna* to raise the finger.

22. After this, send blessings on the Prophet (peace and blessings be upon him) by reciting the *Ṣalāt Ibrāhīmiyya.*

23. Before giving the final *salāms,* it is *sunna* to supplicate. Any short supplication fulfills the *sunna,* though it is best to choose a supplication from the Qur'ān or Sunna.[37]

24. End the prayer by giving *salāms* twice. This is necessary (*wājib*). The *sunna* is to say *As-salāmu ʿalaykum wa raḥmatu 'Llāh* twice, while turning the head (only) to the right for the first and to the left for the second, intending to greet those in prayer with one (even when alone), while specifying the *imām* in one's *salāms* in the direction he is in. It is recommended to turn such that either cheek is pointing back, and to look at the shoulders each time.

The Actions Disliked (*Makrūh*) in the Prayer[38]

The general principles are that:

1. Excessive movement invalidates the prayer
2. Fidgeting is prohibitively disliked (*makrūh taḥrīman*)
3. Slight action or movement not of the prayer is somewhat disliked (*makrūh tanzīhan*), unless it is for a good reason or in the interest of the prayer
4. Omitting a necessary (*wājib*) action is prohibitively disliked (*makrūh taḥrīman*)

5. Leaving a confirmed *sunna* is somewhat disliked (*makrūh tanzīhan*) and blameworthy.

Actions disliked in prayer are:

1. Praying in clothes one would not wear in front of respectable people, (without excuse)
2. Praying in clothes with images of human or animal life is prohibitively disliked, unless the image is very small such that if placed on the floor the features would not be distinctly apparent
3. Yawning[39] or stretching in prayer
4. Praying in a garment one places on one's shoulders without entering the hands in its sleeves
5. Closing one's eyes (unless it helps one's attentiveness, in which case it may even be preferred)
6. A man praying with his head uncovered
7. Pointing one's toes away from the *qibla* in the prostration and sitting
8. Praying while having to relieve oneself is prohibitively disliked. If one feels the definite need to go to the toilet (or pass wind) during the prayer, it is necessary to break the prayer, unless one fears the time of prayer will end
9. Not placing both feet on the ground during prostration, is prohibitively disliked, as placing the toes of one foot is obligatory, and placing the toes of both feet, if only for a moment, is necessary
10. Reciting behind the *imām* (is prohibitively disliked, in any group prayer, whether loud or quiet)

11. Prostrating with one's forehead covered without excuse
12. Raising one's hands when bowing or when standing upright after bowing
13. Praying with one's forearms or shoulders uncovered.[40]

Actions that Invalidate the Prayer

The prayer is invalidated by:

1. Any excessive movement. Excessive movements, which invalidate the prayer, are those that make an onlooker who is unaware that the person is praying think that they are not in the prayer. Eating and drinking are both considered excessive action
2. Speaking with a letter that conveys a meaning or two letters of human speech (regardless of whether it is accidental, intentional, or unintentional)[41]
3. Moaning (by saying *Āh,* or the like) or crying audibly out of remorse or pain. However, if it is out of remembrance of Heaven or Hell, or pain that is unbearable, it does not affect the prayer
4. Coughing without need[42]
5. Moving the chest completely away from the direction of the *qibla* without necessity
6. Reciting from a copy of the Qur'ān
7. Making a grave and inexcusable mistake in recitation that grossly changes the meaning.

The Path to Salvation

It is upon every morally responsible person to keep the following obligations in mind at all times, day and night:

1. Never acting or entering into a transaction without knowing the ruling of Allāh regarding it
2. Eating, drinking and clothing oneself[43] through lawful means[44]
3. Trusting in one's Lord (Exalted is He),[45] being content with His Decree, and thanking Him for all one's blessings
4. Repenting from all sins[46]
5. Being sincere in one's worship, by leaving showing off (*riyā'*) and conceit (*ʿujb*)[47]
6. Not following one's desires, caprice, worldly aspirations, or the whisperings of Satan when these go against the command of Allāh or could lead one towards sin or heedlessness
7. Reciting the Qur'ān, reflecting upon it, and acting upon its teachings

8. Learning the *sunna* of the Beloved of Allāh (Allāh bless him and give him peace), and acting upon its guidance in one's worship, dealings, habits, and adorning oneself with the Prophet's inward states (Allāh bless him and give him peace)[48]
9. Being prepared for death
10. Guarding one's tongue from detestable speech[49]
11. Leaving backbiting, which is to mention someone with that which they dislike, even if it is true. If it is untrue, it is slander, which is a greater sin[50]
12. Commanding the good and forbidding the evil[51]
13. Being good to one's parents[52] and relatives
14. Keeping one's promises
15. Giving in charity to the needy, especially those who are without food
16. Never even coming near fornication (*zinā*).[53]

Appendix 1

The Sunna Prayers: A Detailed Exposition

There are a number of *sunna* prayers associated with each of the obligatory prayers.

Some of these are confirmed *sunnas* and some are non-confirmed *sunnas*.

As for the wisdom in legislating these *sunna* prayers, Imam Ḥaskafī mentions in *al-Durr al-Mukhtār:*

"The *sunna* prayers after the obligatory prayers were legislated to make up for the deficiency in the obligatory prayer, and the *sunna* prayers before the obligatory prayers are to cut off the Devil from his greed."

There are twelve confirmed *sunna* prayers associated with the obligatory prayers.

Umm Ḥabība (Allāh be pleased with her) said, "I heard the Messenger of Allāh (Allāh bless him and give him peace) say 'There is no Muslim servant of Allāh who prays twelve *rakʿat*s besides the obligatory prayer for the sake of Allāh most high except that Allāh makes for him a house in Paradise"' (Muslim). Tirmidhī adds to this in a well and rigorously authenticated narration (*ḥasan ṣaḥīḥ*), "Four before Ẓuhr, two *rakʿat*s after it, two after Maghrib, two after ʿIshā' and two before Fajr."

These twelve *rakʿat*s are:

Two before Fajr
Four before Ẓuhr
Four before and after the Friday prayer
And two after Ẓuhr, Maghrib and ʿIshā'.

Non-confirmed *sunnas* associated with the *farḍ*

Two after Ẓuhr (other than the two confirmed *sunna rakʿat*s offered after Ẓuhr)[53]
Four before ʿAṣr
Six after Maghrib
Four before ʿIshā' and four after ʿIshā'.

[Summarized from an article by Sidi Sohail Hanif.]

Appendix 2

Dealing with Doubts & Misgivings

Severe Doubts & Misgivings

When in such a situation, find out what is the right thing to do, and simply do it. Do not think about the problem or worry about it. Rather, think and thank: think about the blessings of Allāh upon you, and thank Him for them with your tongue and heart. This is a means of making the Devil leave you, and despair of making you despair.

First, exercise caution.

It is important to calmly find out what all the relevant rulings related to the question are. Ask as many specific questions as you have to, and do not make assumptions. Then, figure out what you were doing wrong, if anything, and what the consequences are.

Second, do not have baseless misgivings.

It is essential that one not have baseless misgivings (*waswasa*). This usually occurs due to ignorance of the *sunna,* as operationalized by the *fuqahā'*, or through failure to act within the bounds of sound reason.

As such, we should take the proper means, as described above, and not go beyond them.

Our legal responsibility (*taklīf*) is within the limits of reason: Allāh Most High has informed us, "Allāh does not burden souls with more than they can bear."

Once you have taken the reasonable means, the default assumption is that you are now free from error. Then, we return to the important *fiqh* principle: "Certainty is not vitiated by a doubt" (Ibn Nujaym, *al-Ashbāh wa 'l-naẓā'ir,* and *Majallat al-aḥkām al-ʿadliyya*).

This means that if one is certain about something, such as the validity of one's worship—this being the basic assumption for all human actions—then we continue to assume it is valid until certain that it is not. Mere possibilities and even likelihoods do not change this.

The important *fiqh* principles related to this matter include:

1. Certainty is not lifted by doubt
2. Certainty is only lifted by certainty
3. The default assumption about a matter is akin to certainty
4. The default assumption about all matters is validity and soundness
5. Mere doubts and suppositions are of no legal consequence.

As such, until you are *certain* that any of your prayers were invalid, you do not have any prayers to make up. One should, however, take the steps described above in "exercising caution."

Ibn ʿĀbidīn points out that following one's misgivings (*waswasa*), whether about the validity of one's works or about "how hard" we imagine the legal prescriptions of the Sharīʿa to be is highly blameworthy: it is from the Devil, and Allāh Most High has commanded us to refuse his enticing.

The Prophet (Allāh bless him and give him peace) is a mercy. This religion is a mercy. It is a means to mercy, success, and felicity. When one does not find this, one must be doing something wrong. "Ask the people of remembrance if you know not," Allāh tells us in the Qur'ān.

This is an important final point: when in doubt, one should not make up legal rulings. Rather, one should seek reliable knowledge, either from a reliable book one is able to understand or from people of sound traditional learning.

Appendix 3

Selected Prayers & Sūras

1. Purification:

When beginning ritual ablution, one says,

بِسْمِ اللهِ الرَّحْمٰنِ الرَّحِيْمِ

Bismi 'Llāhi 'r-Raḥmāni 'r-Raḥīm (In the Name of Allāh, Most Merciful and Compassionate)

or

بِسْمِ اللهِ وَالْحَمْدُ لله

Bismi 'Llāh(i), wa 'l-ḥamdu li 'Llāh (In the Name of Allāh, and all praise is due to Allāh).

After ablution one says,

بِسْمِ اللهِ وَالْحَمْدُ لله

Ashhadu al lā ilāha illa 'Llāhu waḥdahū lā sharīka lah(ū), wa ashhadu anna Muḥammadan ʿabduhū wa rasūluh (I bear witness that there is no god but Allāh, One, without partners, and I bear witness that Muḥammad is His servant and messenger)

and

اَللّٰهُمَّ اجْعَلْنِيْ مِنَ التَّوَّابِيْنَ وَاجْعَلْنِيْ مِنَ الْـمُتَطَهِّرِيْنَ

Allāhumma ʾjʿalnī mina ʾt-tawwābīn(a), wa ʾjʿalnī mina ʾl-mutaṭahhirīn (O Allāh, make me of the oft-repentant, and make me of those who have been purified).

2. Prayer

The opening invocation is to say:

سُبْحَانَكَ اللّٰهُمَّ وَبِحَمْدِكَ وَتَبَارَكَ اسْمُكَ وَتَعَالٰى جَدُّكَ وَلَا إِلٰهَ غَيْرُكَ

Subḥānaka ʾLlāhumma wa bi ḥamdik(a), wa tabāraka ʾsmuk(a), wa taʿālā jadduk(a), wa lā ilāha ghayruk (Glory be to You, O Allāh, and all praise. May Your Name be blessed, and Your Might exalted. There is no god but You).

Taʿawwudh is to say:

أَعُوذُ بِاللهِ مِنَ الشَّيْطَانِ الرَّجِيْمِ

A-ʿūdhu bi ʾLlāhi mina ʾsh-shayṭāni ʾr-rajīm (I seek refuge in Allāh from the accursed Devil).

Sūrat al-Fātiḥa:

﴿ بِسْمِ ٱللَّهِ ٱلرَّحْمَٰنِ ٱلرَّحِيمِ ۝١ ٱلْحَمْدُ لِلَّهِ رَبِّ ٱلْعَٰلَمِينَ ۝٢
ٱلرَّحْمَٰنِ ٱلرَّحِيمِ ۝٣ مَٰلِكِ يَوْمِ ٱلدِّينِ ۝٤ إِيَّاكَ نَعْبُدُ وَإِيَّاكَ

نَسۡتَعِينُ ﴿٥﴾ ٱهۡدِنَا ٱلصِّرَٰطَ ٱلۡمُسۡتَقِيمَ ﴿٦﴾ صِرَٰطَ ٱلَّذِينَ أَنۡعَمۡتَ عَلَيۡهِمۡ
غَيۡرِ ٱلۡمَغۡضُوبِ عَلَيۡهِمۡ وَلَا ٱلضَّآلِّينَ ﴿٧﴾

Bismi ’Llāhi r-Raḥmāni ’r-Raḥīm.

Al-ḥamdu li ’Llāhi Rabbi ’l-ʿālamīn(a), Ar-Raḥmāni ’r-Raḥīm(i), Māliki yawmi ’d-dīn(i), iyyāka naʿbudu wa iyyāka nastaʿīn(u), ihdina ’ṣ-ṣirāṭa ’l-mustaqīm(a), ṣirāṭa ’lladhīna anʿamta ʿalayhim ghayri ’l-maghḍūbi ʿalayhim wa la ’ḍḍāllīn.

Short *Sūras*

Al-Ikhlāṣ:

بِسۡمِ ٱللَّهِ ٱلرَّحۡمَٰنِ ٱلرَّحِيمِ

﴿ قُلۡ هُوَ ٱللَّهُ أَحَدٌ ﴿١﴾ ٱللَّهُ ٱلصَّمَدُ ﴿٢﴾ لَمۡ يَلِدۡ وَلَمۡ يُولَدۡ ﴿٣﴾ وَلَمۡ يَكُن لَّهُۥ
كُفُوًا أَحَدُۢ ﴿٤﴾ ﴾

Bismi ’Llāhi r-Raḥmāni r-Raḥīm.

Qul huwa ’Llāhu aḥad(un), Allāhu ’ṣ-ṣamad(u), lam yalid, wa lam yūlad, wa lam yakul lahū kufuwan aḥad.

Al-Falaq:

بِسۡمِ ٱللَّهِ ٱلرَّحۡمَٰنِ ٱلرَّحِيمِ

﴿ قُلۡ أَعُوذُ بِرَبِّ ٱلۡفَلَقِ ﴿١﴾ مِن شَرِّ مَا خَلَقَ ﴿٢﴾ وَمِن شَرِّ غَاسِقٍ إِذَا وَقَبَ
﴿٣﴾ وَمِن شَرِّ ٱلنَّفَّٰثَٰتِ فِي ٱلۡعُقَدِ ﴿٤﴾ وَمِن شَرِّ حَاسِدٍ إِذَا حَسَدَ ﴿٥﴾ ﴾

Bismi ’Llāhi ’r-Raḥmāni ’r-Raḥīm.

Qul a-ʿūdhu bi rabbi ’l-falaq(i), min sharri mā khalaq(a), wa min sharri ghāsiqin idhā waqab(a), wa min sharri 'n-naffāthāti fi 'l-ʿuqad(i), wa min sharri ḥasidin idhā ḥasad.

Al-Nās:

بِسۡمِ ٱللَّهِ ٱلرَّحۡمَٰنِ ٱلرَّحِيمِ

﴿ قُلۡ أَعُوذُ بِرَبِّ ٱلنَّاسِ ١ مَلِكِ ٱلنَّاسِ ٢ إِلَٰهِ ٱلنَّاسِ ٣ مِن شَرِّ
ٱلۡوَسۡوَاسِ ٱلۡخَنَّاسِ ٤ ٱلَّذِي يُوَسۡوِسُ فِي صُدُورِ ٱلنَّاسِ ٥ مِنَ
ٱلۡجِنَّةِ وَٱلنَّاسِ ٦ ﴾

Bismi 'Llāhi 'r-Raḥmāni 'r-Raḥīm.
Qul a-ʿūdhu bi rabbi 'n-nās(i), maliki 'n-nās(i), ilāhi 'n-nās(i), min sharri 'l-waswāsi 'l-khannās(i), alladhī yuwaswisu fī ṣudūri 'n-nās(i), mina 'l-jinnati wa 'n-nās.

Other Invocations

When bowing:

سُبْحَانَ رَبِّيَ الْعَظِيْمِ

Subḥāna Rabbiya 'l-ʿAẓīm (Glory be to my Tremendous Lord).

When rising from bowing:

سَمِعَ اللهُ لِمَنْ حَمِدَهُ

Samiʿa 'Llāhu li man ḥamidah (Allāh hears those who praise Him).

رَبَّنَا لَكَ الْحَمْدُ

Rabbanā laka 'l-ḥamd (O Lord, to You belongs all praise).

When Prostrating:

سُبْحَانَ رَبِّيَ الْأَعْلٰى

Subḥāna Rabbiya 'l-Aʿlā (Glory be to my Lord Most High).

Tashahhud:

اَلتَّحِيَّاتُ لِلّٰهِ وَالصَّلَوَاتُ وَالطَّيِّبَاتُ ، السَّلَامُ عَلَيْكَ أَيُّهَا النَّبِيُّ وَرَحْمَةُ اللهِ وَبَرَكَاتُهُ، ، السَّلَامُ عَلَيْنَا وَعَلٰى عِبَادِ اللهِ الصَّالِحِيْنَ ، أَشْهَدُ أَنْ لَّا إِلٰهَ إِلَّا اللهُ ، وَأَشْهَدُ أَنَّ مُحَمَّدًا عَبْدُهُ، وَرَسُولُهُ،

At-taḥiyyātu li 'Llāhi wa 'ṣ-ṣalawātu wa 'ṭ-ṭayyibāt(u), as-salāmu ʿalayka ayyuha 'n-Nabiyyu wa raḥmatu 'Llāhi wa barakātuh(u), as-salāmu ʿalaynā wa ʿalā ʿibādi 'Llāhi ṣ-ṣāliḥīn(a), ashhadu an lā ilāha illa 'Llāh(u), wa ashhadu anna Muḥammadan ʿabduhū wa rasūluh.

Al-Ṣalāt al-Ibrāhīmiyya:

اَللّٰهُمَّ صَلِّ عَلٰى مُحَمَّدٍ ، وَّعَلٰى آلِ مُحَمَّدٍ كَمَا صَلَّيْتَ عَلٰى إِبْرَاهِيْمَ وَعَلٰى آلِ إِبْرَاهِيْمَ ، وَبَارِكْ عَلٰى مُحَمَّدٍ وَّعَلٰى آلِ مُحَمَّدٍ ، كَمَا بَارَكْتَ عَلٰى إِبْرَاهِيمَ وَعَلٰى آلِ إِبْرَاهِيْمَ ، فِي الْعَالَمِيْنَ إِنَّكَ حَمِيْدٌ مَّجِيْدٌ

Allāhumma ṣalli ʿalā Muḥammadin wa ʿalā āli Muḥammadin kamā ṣallayta ʿalā Ibrāhīma wa ʿalā āli Ibrāhīm(a), wa bārik ʿalā Muḥammadin wa ʿalā āli Muḥammadin kamā bārakta ʿalā Ibrāhīma wa ʿalā āli Ibrāhīm(a), fi 'l-ʿālamīna innaka ḥamīdun majīd.

Short *Duʿā'*

It is especially recommended to use the Prophetic invocations, such as:

اَللّٰهُمَّ إِنِّيْ ظَلَمْتُ نَفْسِيْ ظُلْمًا كَثِيْرًا وَّلَا يَغْفِرُ الذُّنُوْبَ إِلَّا أَنْتَ فَاغْفِرْ لِيْ مَغْفِرَةً مِّنْ عِنْدِكَ وَارْحَمْنِيْ إِنَّكَ أَنْتَ الْغَفُوْرُ الرَّحِيْمُ

Allāhumma innī ẓalamtu nafsī ẓulman kathīra(n), wa lā yaghfiru 'dh-dhunūba illā ant(a), fa 'ghfir lī maghfiratam min ʿindika wa 'rḥamnī, innaka anta 'l-Ghafūru 'r-Raḥīm,

or

يَا مُقَلِّبَ الْقُلُوْبِ ثَبِّتْ قَلْبِيْ عَلٰى دِيْنِكَ

Ya muqalliba 'l-qulūb(i), thabbit qalbī ʿalā dīnik.

Extra:

رَبِّ اغْفِرْ لِيْ وَلِوَالِدَيَّ ، رَبِّ ارْحَمْهُمَا كَمَا رَبَّيَانِيْ صَغِيْرًا

Rabbi 'ghfir lī wa li wālidayy(a), Rabbi 'rḥamhumā kamā rabbayānī ṣaghīrā.

Notes

1. His Will and Power are related to all rationally possible things. His Power brings into being that which is specified by His Will (in accordance with His Knowledge).
2. The worth of actions is weighed on the Scale. The intellect is unable to understand its true nature. The wisdom behind the Scale is to test the slave's belief in the Unseen, to make reward and punishment known to him, and to establish a proof for or against him.
3. The Path is a bridge over the Fire that the people of Heaven will cross, while the people of Hell will slip and fall into the Fire. In his *Iḥyā' ʿulūm al-dīn,* Imam Ghazālī (may Allāh have mercy on him) mentions that those who remain upright on the straight path in this world will be able to cross over the Path in the Afterlife and be saved, whereas those who leave uprightness in this world and burden their souls with sins will slip on their first step and fall off.
4. The Questioning takes place in the grave by the two questioning angels, Munkar and Nakīr.
5. Decisively established texts are the entire Qur'ān, and those ḥadīths related by multiple contiguous chains (*mutawātir*).
6. Being wasteful in using the permitted is blameworthy and can even become sinful if excessive.
7. If any clearly perceptible barrier such as paint, nail polish, or candle

wax remains on the skin, it prevents water from reaching the skin, and leads to an incomplete ritual bath or ablution. Similarly, if even a small amount of skin remains unwashed, the ritual bath or ablution is not valid.

8. One intends either to perform the ritual bath or to become ritually pure. An intention is that the heart resolves to do something. Formally, it is to firmly resolve to perform an action, and to draw closer to Allāh, when initiating the action. It should be noted that there are three aspects to the intention: (1) the minimum legally valid intention, which is to firmly resolve to perform an action; (2) intention needed for reward, which is to also intend to draw closer to Allāh; (3) the time: it is a condition that the intention be made as one initiates the action, or just before it.
9. Filth (*najāsa*) includes anything that comes out of the private parts, blood, pus, and vomit that is more than a mouthful. It is necessary to remove any filth on one's body or clothes. Filth is removed by washing it until no trace of it remains.
10. This Qur'ānic verse established the obligatory acts of ritual ablution. Everything else, that is *sunna* or recommended, was established through the practice of the Beloved Messenger of Allāh (Allāh bless him and give him peace).
11. It is not necessary to pronounce the intention, but if pronouncing it helps to bring the intention to mind, then it is recommended.
12. Brushing one's teeth in ablution is an emphasized *sunna*. It is optimally done with a tooth-stick (*miswāk*), though the basic *sunna* would also be fulfilled by a toothbrush. Brushing one's teeth is also recommended before the prayer; if the teeth are yellow; if one's breath changes; before meeting people; and for reading the Qur'ān or sacred knowledge. One should hold the tooth-stick in one's right hand. If one does not have access to a tooth-stick or brush, one should use a coarse cloth or one's fingers.
13. For the condition of "washing" to be fulfilled, it is necessary that water drip from the washed limb, even if only a drop or two. Ibn ʿĀbidīn cautions, however, that this merely defines the minimum and that it

is disliked to use very little water, such that it resembles wiping rather than washing.

14. It is disliked to wipe the head more than once with new water.

15. When in a rush, it is better to perform all the *sunnas* once rather than some of them three times.

16. Anything filthy that comes out of the private parts invalidates the ritual ablution as soon as it appears on the surface of the body. From other than the private parts, the ritual ablution is only invalidated if filth flows past its point of exit (such as a wound), or *would* have flowed had it not been wiped away.

17. If one sleeps with one's rear firmly seated, one's ritual ablution is not invalidated.

18. Laughing out loud is defined as being such that another could hear the laughter. Laughing such that only oneself can hear it invalidates the prayer, but does not necessitate ritual ablution. Laughing in the funeral prayer or during a prostration of recital (*tilāwa*) or thanksgiving (*shukr*) invalidates the prayer or prostration but does not necessitate ritual ablution.

19. Intercourse, even without ejaculation, makes a ritual bath (*ghusl*) obligatory.

20. For women this also means not being in a state of menstruation. The minimum period of menstruation is three days, the maximum ten days. It is personally obligatory for women to know the essential rulings related to menstruation.

21. The excused amount of filth is the extent of one's inner palm, which is approximately 5 cm in diameter. Filth is removed by washing it away. Other ways are explained in lengthier texts.

22. The soundest opinion is that it is not obligatory for a woman to cover her feet. However, the more cautious opinion is that she should cover them, especially for the prayer.

23. There should be no undue interruption between the intention and the opening invocation (*takbīr,* which is to say *Allāhu akbar,* "Allāh is greatest") by any action unrelated to the prayer.

If the prayer is supererogatory, an unconditioned intention is sufficient; such as "I intend to pray." This also applies for emphasized *sunna* prayers, though it is best to specify what one is praying; such as "I intend to pray the *sunna* of Maghrib." The place of the intention is the heart; it is recommended to pronounce it when this helps one focus.

For obligatory prayers, one must specify the prayer, though not the number of *rakʿats;* e.g. "I intend to pray the obligatory Maghrib prayer."

What counts in the intention is the action of the heart, such that one knows without hesitation or doubt what one is praying. Pronouncing the intention is recommended (*mustaḥabb*), if it aids the heart.

24. It is permitted to pray sitting in other than the obligatory and necessary prayers. But this has half the reward of praying standing, unless one is unable to pray standing. The exception is the *sunna* of Fajr, which one must stand for if able, according to Abū Ḥanīfa (may Allah have mercy on him). Some scholars also consider it necessary to stand for Tarāwīḥ prayers.

25. Standing is necessary for the one able to stand and prostrate. If one can stand but not prostrate, it is recommended to pray sitting and motion with the head.

26. This is the minimum recitation required for the prayer to be valid. One must, however, recite the necessary (*wājib*) amount. According to the soundest opinion, it is necessary that one be able to hear one's voice in order to be validly reciting. According to a more lenient, though sound opinion, the minimally valid recitation is to pronounce the letters by moving one's lips, even if no actual sound is made. It is best only to use this latter opinion retroactively, to avoid making up past prayers. The scholars note, however, that there is no difference of opinion that mere "thinking" is not considered valid recitation. Therefore, it is obligatory to repeat prayers performed without even moving the lips for recitation.

27. If a necessary action of the prayer is omitted, the prayer is not invalidated, though it is necessary to repeat it. If a necessary action is left out of forgetfulness, it can be made up by two forgetfulness prostrations at the end of the prayer. These two prostrations are performed after one

salām. After them, one must repeat the final sitting, including its invocations, *tashahhud* and prayers on the Prophet (Allāh bless him and give him peace). One finishes, as in a normal prayer, with two *salāms*.

28. It is also necessary (*wājib*) to remain motionless for a moment when standing after bowing, and in the sitting between the two prostrations, according to a strong position.

29. It is also necessary (*wājib*), in the *witr* prayer to recite the invocation of *witr* (*qunūt*). Its place is before bowing after making a *takbīr:* by saying *Allāhu akbar* and raising one's hands as in the beginning of the prayer. The *witr* prayer is a three *rakʿa* prayer in which one must recite both the Fātiḥa and some verses in all three *rakʿat*s. Its time is after the night prayer (ʿIshā').

30. According to a more lenient, though sound opinion, the minimally valid recitation is to pronounce the letters by moving one's lips, even if no actual sound is made.

31. Such as four fingers apart, or as comfortable in a reasonably close manner.

32. Pronounce the opening invocation (*taḥrīma*) with the tongue, such that you can hear yourself, after having made the intention. Saying the opening invocation or the obligatory recitation in one's mind without actually uttering it with one's tongue is insufficient and renders one's prayer invalid.

33. There must not be an undue gap: speech, eating, and any action that invalidates the prayer, between the intention and opening invocation. All actions of the prayer relate to pronouncing with the tongue, except intention.

34. It is prohibitively disliked (*makrūh taḥrīman*) for the follower to recite the Fātiḥa or Qur'ān behind the *imām*.

35 Such as *witr, sunna,* and voluntary prayers.

36. Namely, necessary, *sunna,* and voluntary prayers.

37. When supplicating with one's own words, it is necessary that the supplication not resemble common human speech, which is defined as being anything it is normally possible to ask of humans. If one supplicates

with something normally possible to ask of humans (such as, "O Allāh, marry me to Zayd,") it invalidates the prayer. It is improper to supplicate in other than Arabic.

38. Unless mentioned otherwise these actions are somewhat disliked (*makrūh tanzīhan*).

39. If yawning overcomes one, one should cover the mouth to restrain it. It is prohibitively disliked if done intentionally without need, in the prayer, and is somewhat disliked outside the prayer.

40. If one's sleeves are rolled up, it is best to unfold them with slight movements. Similarly, if one's cap falls off, it is best to pick it up and put it back on, if this is possible to do with only slight movements.

41. This includes greeting others and answering their greetings, laughter, and any *dhikr* or Qur'ānic verses recited with the intention of addressing another person.

42. Need includes discomfort, clearing one's throat, or improving one's ability to recite or supplicate.

43. Note that silk is permitted for women, not men. Men cannot adorn themselves with gold or silver: except for a silver ring and sword adornment, if the intention is not adornment. Neither men nor women can use gold and silver utensils.

44. This includes knowing the *fiqh* of the *ḥalāl* and *ḥarām,* and of transactions, and asking reliable scholars when uncertain.

45. Trusting in one's Lord means that one does not hope except from Him, and fears none but Him. Trust is one of the five things through which the Path of the Sufis is sought, as mentioned by Ibn ʿArabī. These five things are: trust in Allāh, certainty, patience, determination, and being true. So it is upon the intelligent to consign all their affairs to Allāh, and not to rely on others, for Allāh Most High says, "And whosoever puts their trust in Allāh, He will suffice him" (Qur'ān 65:3).

46. The conditions for a valid repentance are four: remorse for having disobeyed Allāh; leaving the sin; determining never to return to it; and to mend any grievances (such as money owed to others, or making up unperformed acts of worship).

47. Allāh Most High told us, "And whoever hopes for the meeting with his Lord, let him do righteous work, and make none share in the worship due unto his Lord" (Qur'ān 18:110).

48. The way to live the *sunna* of the Beloved of Allāh (Allāh bless him and give him peace) and to bring light and meaning to one's life is by learning and following one of the four Sunni schools of *fiqh*. They are means of operationalizing the guidance of the Qur'ān and Sunna step by step, without the excesses of extremism or laxity.

49. This includes leaving any jest that contravenes the Sacred Law, especially mocking others and sarcasm.

50. Backbiting can be explicit with the tongue, or by actions such as mimicry. If one fell into backbiting and it did not reach the other person, then it is enough to feel remorse and repent. Otherwise, one would have to inform the person and seek their forgiveness, as well, unless one fears that this would cause problems or worsen relations.

51. The good is that which conforms to the Sacred Law and the bad is that which contravenes it. It is only necessary to command good and forbid evil if one believes that the person will listen. If one thinks that the person will not listen, it is not necessary; however, it is better to advise that person, even if it entails harm to one. But, if the person becomes worse or more entrenched in their wrongdoing because of this, it is better to remain silent. Enjoining the good and forbidding the evil needs to be done in a gentle and mild way, and in private whenever possible.

52. "Your Lord has decreed that you worship none save Him, and [that you show] kindness to parents" (Qur'ān 18:23). The command to be good to one's parents is absolute. Even when exercising one's rights, one must be respectful to one's parents and speak to them accordingly.

53. This includes lowering one's gaze, and avoiding looking or listening to anything unlawful.

53. These two *rakʿat*s can be offered after the two confirmed *sunna rakʿat*s that are offered after the Ẓuhr prayer or together with them as one four *rakʿa* prayer with one *salām* (Ibn ʿĀbidīn, *Radd al-muḥtār*).

About the Author

Sidi Faraz Rabbani is a student of Ḥanafī *fiqh* and the Islamic sciences. After graduating from the University of Toronto with a degree in Commerce and Economics, he spent three years in Damascus where he studied *fiqh*, *ʿaqīda*, and other subjects with Shaykh Adīb al-Kallās, Shaykh Ḥassān al-Hindī, Shaykh Muḥammad Jumuʿa, Shaykh Muḥammad Qaylīsh, Shaykh Mu'min al-ʿAnnān, and others.

He then moved to Amman in the summer of 2000, where he has lived since then, continuing his studies with teachers in Jordan, and corresponding regularly with scholars in the Indian Subcontinent. Sidi Faraz is a student of Shaykh Nuh Keller and teaches Ḥanafī *fiqh* and other subjects in Amman and through Sunni Path (www.SunniPath.com), an online center for Islamic knowledge.

Also by

White Thread Press

Provisions for the Seekers

Sufism & Good Character

The Differences of the Imams

Prayers for Forgiveness: Seeking Spiritual Enlightenment through Sincere Supplication

Fiqh al-Imam: Key Proofs in Hanafi Fiqh

Reflections of Pearls

The Laws of Animal Slaughter

Imam Abu Hanifa's Al-Fiqh al-Akbar with Maghnisawi's Commentary

The Book of Perfection (Tasawwuf)

White Thread Press, (first founded as Prudence Publications in the UK) is a publisher of traditional Islamic texts based in Santa Barbara, California. Its mission is to aid in the revival of the true heritage of scholarship in the Muslim Umma, and to fill the educational and spiritual needs of contemporary Muslims in the English-speaking world, by presenting, in the English language, original works by contemporary scholars and translated classical texts of scholars past.

May Allāh accept our endeavors and grant us guidance and success.

Give the gift of

Absolute Essentials of Islam

to your friends and colleagues

Ask at Your Local Islamic Bookstore or Order Here

[ ] Yes, I want____copies of *Absolute Essentials of Islam* for the special price of $7.95 each (RRP 8.95).

Include $1.95 for shipping and handling for one book, and $0.95 for each additional book. Ohio residents must include applicable sales tax. Canadian orders must include payment in US funds. Payment must accompany orders. Allow two weeks for delivery.

My check or money order for $_______ is enclosed.
Please charge my
[ ]Visa [ ]Mastercard [ ]American Express [ ]Discover

Name ____
Organization ___________________________________
Address ______________________________________
City/State/Zip _________________________________
Phone ______________ E-Mail ___________________
Card ____
Exp. Date ____________ Signature _________________

Fax (309) 273 1844 or e-mail your order to info@whitethreadpress.com
Also order online at www.whitethreadpress.com

Optionally mail completed order form with payment to
Al-Rashad Books
3340 Hunter Parkway
Cuyahoga Falls, OH 44223
805 968 4666

UK orders. Please contact Azhar Academy Ltd
sales@azharacademy.com or call 020 8534 9191